The Gospel of the
Rainbow
Sign

Other books by Howard W. Boldt:

The Real Biblical Elder (2018) ISBN 9781773540672
Judge For Yourselves (2021) ISBN 9781773543642
The Cure For Pentecostalism (2021) ISBN 9781773543635

The Gospel of the
Rainbow
Sign

He who sheds man's blood,
By Man shall His blood be shed

Howard W. Boldt

THE GOSPEL OF THE RAINBOW SIGN
He who sheds Man's blood, By Man shall His blood be shed.

Published by Howard Boldt, Edmonton, Canada

ISBN 978-1-77354-066-5

Publication assistance and digital printing in Canada by

PAGEMASTER
PUBLISHING
PageMaster.ca

TABLE OF CONTENTS

Preface v

1.   Introduction.. 1

2.   The Sacrifices 3

3.   God's Imperatives.. 7

4.   The 'Required' Inspections... 15

5.   God's Three Inspections 17

6.   The Sacrifice and Priest.. 25

7.   The Image of God.. 31

8.   The Two Covenants... 35

9.   The Gospel Covenant 39

10. Notes... 47

Preface

Virtually every commentary of Genesis nine teach that God is laying the foundation of human government to Noah. It is universally held today that 'whoso sheds man's blood by man shall his blood be shed', pertains to the right of the state to practice capital punishment. (Gen. 9:6a) However, this is not an imperative. As I pondered this entire portion of Scripture, it became evident that this was not about governmental authority at all.

Because the interpretation of this book is likely unknown to the reader, the first impulse is to reject it out of hand. After all, 'how is it possible for right teaching on a Scripture passage such as this, be unknown?' This question presumes that a right view, on a passage such as this, must be known. Rather, as the author of this book, I contend that any right view, except for unfulfilled prophecies, have been previously known. Since all published commentary on Scriptures is not correct, it is feasible that all known commentary of one passage of Scripture, such as Gen. 9:5, 6, is incorrect. A published view does not make it a correct view. Neither are all right views of Scripture published. Therefore, if the exposition of this book is biblical, I am certainly not the first person to have known it.

The Bereans were good examples of how to approach something 'new'. Never before had they heard that their prophesied Savior had died and risen from the dead for their sins, so they searched the Scriptures to verify Paul's message. This was new! Like the Bereans, I urge the reader to evaluate my commentary by asking, 'Is this 'new' to Scripture?'

It is my hope that God's words to Noah shortly after he left the Ark, will increase your appreciation of Christ's work at the cross of Calvary, as it did mine.

Howard Boldt

ABBREVIATIONS

New King James Version quotations are designated NKV.
New American Standard quotations are designated NAS
Young's Literal Translation quotations are designated YLT

1. INTRODUCTION

The Genesis account of the Flood is an amazing story familiar to Christianized society. However, as with the creation narrative, to most of professing Christianity today, the worldwide Flood is just another novel. One survey conducted over a decade ago showed that among conservative Christian academia, only 58% believed that the Flood was worldwide, and about a similar percentage believed that the world was created in six literal 24 hour days.[1]

Different from the biblical account, flood legends are plentiful. Tablets discovered in Iraq record a story of a worldwide where *Ea* told *Upnapishtim* to build a boat to save his family. The North American Indians, Australian Aboriginals, Chinese, Egypt, Peru, Scandinavia and others also have various versions of how a few people were saved from a catastrophic flood.[2] Multiple similar accounts of a catastrophy such as this among unrelated people groups today, do indicate the reality of a historical event. But, as with all recorded history, they are not Holy Spirit- inspired accounts and therefore, subject to error.

Sadly, professing Christendom, for the most part has rejected the inspired biblical narrative of the Flood, not to mention Creation. What were once evangelical Christian churches and colleges, have replaced biblical authority with their own. By denying the Flood, they profess to know more than Isaiah, who compared the reality of the Covenant to the reality of the Flood. (Is. 54:9, 10) They profess to know more than Peter, who sat under the teaching of Christ. (1 Pe. 3:20, 21; 2 Pe. 3:5, 6) Jesus emphasized the reality of a future judgment of death by referencing Noah's flood as an historical event. (Matt. 24:36-39) By denying the reality of the Flood, professing

---

[1] Ken Ham & Greg Hall, *Already Compromised*, 2011, p. 52-54
https://assets.answersingenesis.org/doc/articles/am/v6/n3/already-comp-ch3.pdf
[2] Flood, A wealth Of Deluge Legends, by Rebecca Conolly and Russell Grigg
https://creation.com/many-flood-legends

Christendom impugn the integrity of Isaiah, the Apostle Peter and Christ Himself.

After the ark had settled on Mt. Ararat, Noah convened a worship service. (Ge. 8:20) This ritual is part of the story of the Flood. Did Noah figuratively land on the mountain; did he figuratively build an altar unto the Lord and offer a figurative sacrifice on it? Besides the explicit statement that the waters had risen to a height of 17 cubits above the mountains, there are other elements of this record that necessitates an historical perspective. (Ge. 7:20)

At this worship service, God Noah is reminded of a Covenant He had made for mankind. Was this Covenant non-literal also? However, if the altar and the sacrifice were literal, then the Promise of the Covenant must also be literal, that is, point forward to a yet future historical transaction. Not only is a fulfilled Covenant evidence of a promise-keeping God, it also bears witness to the reality of the events in which it was given.

The Covenant God affirmed with Noah is the same Covenant He initiated, when Adam and Eve sinned in Eden. If this Covenant was fulfilled in human history, then the circumstances in which it was first given and later affirmed must also be literal. So, finally, after centuries of literal forbearance, God's literal wrath reaches its limit, and with the exception of Noah and his family, all human life is literally destroyed with a literal flood.

Despite Noah finding grace in the eyes of the Lord, he and his family were still sinners. The Covenant God made with our first parents was still the only means of deliverance from sin, including Noah. It was while he was worshipping God with sacrifices, that He informed Noah in greater detail how that would be accomplished.

Sin's punishment is death, literal spiritual death. (Rom. 6:23)

God smelled a soothing aroma.

2. The Sacrifices

Grieved by man's wickedness, God determined to blot man including animals, from earth. But, Noah had found grace in the eyes of the Lord and was spared this awful fate. Trusting God for deliverance from the fate of his wicked generation, Noah obediently built the ark as instructed. (Ge. 6:5-8; 14-16, 22) Finally finished, after more than a century, God invited Noah and his family into the ark, with a male and female of each kind of animal and bird. Seven days after they had entered the ark, it started to rain, which continued for forty days and nights. They would remain on the ark for over a year.

As Noah scanned the Ararat landscape from the window of the ark, he must have had an eerie feeling. Except for the passengers on the ark, the Flood God promised destroyed all human and animal life. Unrepentant mockers may have even assisted Noah with the construction of this 'crazy' boat, but despite their 'good works', rejected Noah's preaching. (2 Pe. 2:5) Commerce, carousing and the mocking had all come to an unexpected, yet prolonged ending, until the last person was finally overwhelmed with the waters of judgment.

After the waters had abated and the land was sufficiently dried, God commanded Noah and his family to leave the ark and bring out with him all the birds and animals. And, as God told Adam and Eve, He also commanded Noah to be 'fruitful and multiply' upon the earth. (Ge. 1:28; 8:16, 17)

NOAH WORSHIPED GOD

Noah did not forget his gracious God. Shortly after leaving the ark, Noah offered burnt sacrifices to the Lord. This was not a memorial service to remember the lives of drowned humanity! But this was a memorial service to worship One who would come to die, according God's Covenant with Noah! (Ge. 8:20)

THE SOOTHING AROMA

On this momentous occasion Noah offers blood sacrifices to the Lord, with which God was pleased. God smelled a soothing aroma. He then promised that for man's sake, He would never curse the ground again. (Ge. 8:21)

By faith, Noah knew that God was pleased with the shedding of blood. Only by the death of another could he be delivered from his sin. His own works were not acceptable.

But why did God smell a soothing aroma? (Ge. 8:20, 21) Noah knew which animals God considered clean. Like the Mosaic regulations for sacrifices, the health, lack of deformity, and the kind of animal symbolized the character and perfection God required for an acceptable sacrifice. Noah obediently sacrificed an animal he knew was 'clean'. He knew that God had been displeased with Cain's offering but had 'respect' for Abel's, because he had sacrificed the firstborn of his flock of sheep.

But was the essence of God's pleasure simply that Noah had offered the right kind of animal? Since we know that God did not take pleasure in burnt offerings, the reason for the 'soothing aroma' was not the animal sacrifice itself. (Heb. 10:6, 8) God begins to explain exactly why He smelled 'a soothing aroma.'

GOD'S FIRST SACRIFICES

The sacrificial system began with God. Noah's worship service was not a human innovation.

After Adam and Eve disobeyed God, they suddenly discovered that they were naked. Now ashamed, they attempted to hide from God. They clothed themselves with fig leaves they had sewn together. But these first attempts, to reconcile themselves to God with a garment of their own works, utterly failed. God was not pleased with their works.

When God provided animal skins to cover the nakedness of Adam and Eve, He demonstrated that to expiate sin innocent life needed to be offered. (Ge. 3:21) Not having done anything wrong, these animals died because of someone else's sin. With this first sacrifice God demonstrated that Adam and Eve needed a blood sacrifice.

MAN'S FIRST SACRIFICES

After Eden, two sons of Adam and Eve bear witness to rejected and acceptable worship.

CAIN'S SACRIFICE

Cain brought an offering to the Lord of the 'fruit of the ground'. (Gen. 4:2, 3) Without a doubt, Cain would have known about the necessity that an acceptable sacrifice required the life of a 'clean' animal. Yet in rebellion, Cain innovated his worship by introducing a bloodless sacrifice. Obviously, he reasoned that atoning death for his sin was not necessary.

ABEL'S SACRIFICE

Abel, however, brought the first born of a flock of sheep. Because this was a blood sacrifice, God accepted it.

SUMMARY

Having trusted a bloodless sacrifice of his own works, that could not cover his sin, God warned Cain that sin is waiting to pounce upon him. Rather than depend upon God for his good works, he trusted himself. Unable to deliver himself from sin, Cain murdered his brother. (Ge. 4:7) On the other hand, Abel offered the required sacrifice, showing that he trusted God to deliver him from his sin. Cain trusted in himself. Abel trusted in the life of another to expiate his sin.

To live right, man must worship right.

THE DILEMMA

However, this Priest of Eden, likely the pre-incarnate Christ, perfectly holy and righteous, had not offered an adequate sacrifice for Adam and Eve. Had the sacrifice of animals been sufficient, it would not have to be constantly repeated. Noah would certainly have surmised that the animal sacrifices made by God Himself for

Adam and Eve were insufficient, that sinful man could not possibly make the final sacrifice for sin.

Man would repeat this blood ritual that God began in the Garden of Eden as a reminder of the costly penalty for sin and the means of redemption. This was the first means of worship. Only by admitting that he is incapable of paying for his sin, and by faith receive the blood sacrifice for his redemption, can man truly worship.

God knew, of course, that His animal sacrifices in the Garden of Eden would be insufficient. They were only intended to begin teaching mankind essential features of a future and final sacrifice needed to restore fellowship with God that Adam and Eve had lost in the Garden of Eden.

Abel's offering was accepted and Noah's offering was a soothing aroma. Why? The answer to this question is answered for us in Noah's first worship service after the Flood.

3. God's Imperatives

God commands and informs Noah further regarding propagation, work, authority, food and sacrifices.

> "So God blessed Noah and his sons, and said to them: 'Be fruitful and multiply, and fill the earth. And the fear of you and the dread of you shall be on every beast of the earth and on the fish of the sea. They are given into your hand. Every moving thing that lives shall be food for you. I have given you all things even as the green herbs. But you shall not eat flesh with its life, that is, its blood." (Gen.9:1-4; NKJV)

It is important to keep the context in mind. Noah had been offering animal sacrifices. During this worship service, God blessed Noah and his sons. For the sake of distinguishing His imperatives, the first three are denoted as 'commands' and the last one a 'prohibition'.

The Three Commands

God commanded Noah to be fruitful and multiply and replenish the earth. (9:1) God had also said these same words to Adam and Eve. (Ge. 1:28) However, these words do not mean the same thing. Therefore, these words do not all refer to the propagation of the human race.

Bear Fruit

God ordered Noah and his family to work, to prosper.

God promised Abram that he would become exceedingly fruitful. (Ge. 17:5, 6) As a father of many nations this context defines fruitful as plentiful progeny. But in other contexts, fruitful pertains to prosperity derived from meaningful labor and ability.

Rather than struggle with competing herdsmen for water, Isaac opted to dig another well. Thus God had also made room for Isaac to be fruitful in the land. 'Fruitful' indicates that Isaac would prosper in the land by means of his livestock. (Ge. 26:20-22)

Isaac charged his son Jacob to take a wife from the daughters of Laban. Isaac blessed his son, 'May God bless you and make you fruitful and multiply you.' (Ge. 28:1-3) Isaac pronounced a twofold blessing upon Jacob: that he would prosper (bear fruit) in the livestock business, and that he would have children. (Ge. 30:37-43)

Joseph named one of his sons Ephraim as a reminder that God had made fruitful in the land of affliction, a clear reference to the food he had gathered during the seven years of plenty. (Ge. 41:47, 51-53)

In Egypt the children of Israel were gainfully employed. They were fruitful. (Ge. 47:27) Jacob blesses his grandsons Ephraim and Manasseh that God would make them fruitful and multiply them. Similar to previous passages, God gives them the ability to prosper in their work.

To be fruitful meant that man was to provide for his physical. When Adam and Eve ate of the forbidden fruit, they were unfruitful. (Ge.47:27)

Multiply

As noted in the scripture referenced above, there is a distinct difference between "fruitful" and "multiply".

God ordered Noah's family to have children, to multiply. It is noteworthy that God gave this command to married couples! At creation, God gave this command to Adam and Eve; at Ararat God gave this command to four men, each with his own wife.

Fill the Earth

God commanded Noah to 'fill the earth'. Perhaps the first clue to understanding this command is found in the narrative of Babel.

> "And they said, Go to, let us build us a city and a tower, whose top may reach unto heaven; and let us make us a name, lest we be scattered abroad upon the face of the whole earth." (Ge. 11:4; KJV)

Rather than obey God's command to fill the earth, they intentionally built a city to do the exact opposite. By confusing their language, God stopped their city building project and scattered them upon all the face of the earth. (Ge. 11:8, 9)

Summary

Noah was commanded to be prosperous, to multiply and to fill the whole earth. God had ordained the means by which humanity could flourish socially.

THE PROHIBITION

God informed Noah of what appears to be a new challenge of animal fear of man. Yet, animals were given into man's hand, that is, man had power over them. (Ge. 9:1-2) Any living thing could now be food for them. However, eating the blood of the flesh was forbidden.

Man was commanded not to eat the representation of life, the blood of animals. (Lev. 17:10, 11, 14; De.12:16, 17, 23, 24) One reason for heeding this prohibition is borne out by what this practice invariably leads to. By the eating of blood, even Israel was led into vile practices of various forms of Satan worship. (Lev.19:26)

The basic reason for this prohibition was that blood represented life. (Lev. 17:11) God reserved blood to represent the life of man. So, blood had become the new forbidden 'food'. When Adam and Eve ate of the prohibited fruit, they died. Extricated from Eden, they had no access to the Tree of Life. However, God provided mankind with 'food' from the fruit of another Tree, without which man die in his sins. That 'food' came from another 'tree' of Life, the cross of Christ. (Jn. 6:53, 54; Col. 1:20; 1 Pe. 2:24)

A PRESUMED COMMAND

There is no doubt that verses one to three contain imperatives, not suggestions. But in verses five and six, it is presumed that Noah was given a command regarding capital punishment. The actual meaning of these verses will be discussed in later chapters, but for now it is important to show why these verses do not pertain to governing authorities for the punishment of murderers.

COMMENTARY DEFORMATION

Note how the context is warped when verse six is viewed as an imperative for capital punishment. One commentator connects verses 6 and 7 as follows,

> "Instead of taking away the lives of men, the great concern should be to multiply them; and this indeed is one reason for the above law, to prevent the decrease and ruin of mankind; and which was peculiarly needful, when there were so few men in the world as only four and therefore it is repeated in stronger terms."[3]

Despite the violence of the antediluvians, this generation had no problem in populating the earth without this censure, so it's incongruent to teach that after the flood murder would interfere with God's command to replenish the earth.

Cain, the Murderer

God put a protecting mark on Cain to prevent vengeance on his life. The view that murder would somehow interfere with repopulating the earth doesn't hold up, since Cain had a wife and family after killing Abel, thus helping to populate the earth. Had God intended to change the penal code for Noah, the command would have been explicit. There is no logical context to link murder and execution with the propagation of the race.

The presumption that verses five and six are commands for Noah to execute the murderer introduces an artificial context.

Who is Commanded?

With the words, 'I will examine', God identifies Himself as one who is doing the work. (9:5) There is no change in verse six. It is after verse six that God specifically addresses "you", which are Noah and his family. 'You be fruitful' is a specific command stating who

---

[3] *John Gill's Exposition of the Whole Bible*, Gen. 9:7 The 'above law' refers to his belief that verse six is a command not to murder.

should do what. (9:7) When God says, 'as for Me, I confirm My Covenant', He states what He will do. (9:8)

Presumptuous commentary notwithstanding, the subject of the narrative has actually changed from a promise in verse six to a command in verse seven. (9:6, 7) This is the 'My Covenant' God promises in verse 8.

"As for you", clearly implies that what was just stated, was not something Noah could do. He could, however, be fruitful, multiply and replenish the earth. God would take care of the promise in verse six; Noah would obey God with the command in verses one and seven.

THE 'COMMAND' PRESUMPTION CHALLENGED

The command God gives in verse seven is in fact similar to the one he gave earlier. "And as for you ..." 'You, Noah, be fruitful and multiply and replenish the earth.' (Gen. 9:1,7)

But it is presumed by virtually every commentary that 'require' means 'kill' and that 'he who sheds man's blood, by man shall his blood be shed...' is a command to execute the murderer. (9:5, 6) Note the following challenges to this view:

The Dictionary Challenge

The word for 'require' in verse five means to inspect, or tread upon. The capital punishment view redefines the Hebrew word to mean kill. None of the meanings for the Hebrew word for 'require' even imply the meaning of 'kill', or 'murder'. (Brown-Driver-Briggs)

Grammatical Challenge

Though the grammatical construction of verses six and seven stand in sharp contrast, commentators still presume both to be commands. If verse six is really a command as verse seven is, then transposing the grammar of verse six onto verse seven should not alter the meaning. Indeed, 'Be fruitful and multiply and bring forth abundantly in the earth' is clearly a command, but note how the imperative vanishes when this verse is edited to parallel verse 6,

'He who replenishes the earth, by him shall the earth be replenished.' or, 'Those who populate the earth, by them shall the earth be repopulated.' or, 'As for you who multiply in the earth, by him shall the earth be multiplied therein.'

The verse is no longer an imperative; it becomes informative and predictive. This verse now states that the entire earth will be replenished by him who replenishes. Now, similar to verse 6, there is no command.

'Every Man's Brother' Challenge

Another insurmountable challenge, of course, is the connection of verse six to verse five, discussed later. The 'man' in verse 6 is identified in the previous verse as 'every man's brother.'

The Context Challenge

The capital punishment interpretation completely ignores the context. Noah was offering burnt offerings.

The Example Challenge

Cain murdered his brother, but God did not kill him. He was punished certainly, but not killed. Had God not identified Cain with a protecting mark, it is implied that someone would have taken his life. From Cain's fear of being killed for taking Abel's life, it seems that the antediluvians knew that just law required 'an eye for an eye and a tooth for a tooth'.

David killed Uriah yet God did not demand David's life. Saul participated in killing Christians like Stephen, yet God did not demand his death.

SCRIPTURE FOR CAPITAL PUNISHMENT

The Mosaic Law detailed situations that required the death sentence, murder being just one of them. (Ex. 21:28, 29) In a subject so important as retributive justice, God left us with clear statements for capital punishment. (Nu. 35:16-21; De. 19:10-13)

Governmental authorities have the God-given right to take the life of a murderer. (Rom. 13:4) But God's commandments and promise to Noah in this passage is not about establishing human government. It's about how God would provide His remedy for sin.

MURDER WAS ONLY ONE 'MAJOR' SIN.

The whole Law, being transcendent, was known by this sinful generation as evidenced by the lives of Enoch and Noah. God flooded the world because of that generation's wickedness, that every thought and intent of the heart was continually evil. (Ge. 6:5) If all the murders were executed, the world would still be a lawless place.

SUMMARY

Nothing in verses five and six even remotely suggest capital punishment. If someone had just been murdered, we might expect God to say something about that to Noah. But this was a worship service, not a crime scene. Genesis 9:6 is framed as a promise or prophecy, which, in this narrative, is referred to as "My Covenant".

Spoken to Noah in a worship service in which animal blood was shed, this promise also highlights the shedding of blood.

4. The 'Required' Inspections

Because God's holiness cannot tolerate the presence of sin, man's status is exceedingly precarious. Man's blood must be tested.

"Surely for your lifeblood I will demand a reckoning; from the hand of every beast will I require it; and from the hand of man. From the hand of every man's brother will I require the life of man. Whoever sheds man's blood, by man his blood shall be shed; for in the image of God he made man. And as for you, be fruitful and multiply; bring forth abundantly in the earth, and multiply in it." (Gen. 9:5-7; NKJ)

THE MEANING OF 'REQUIRE'

The Hebrew word for 'require' means to 'tread' or to 'frequent'. It can also mean to 'make inquisition' or to 'search out'. Any of these meanings can be taken without interfering with the context. A different form of the word *durash* is also translated as 'reckoning',

"Reuben answered the saying, "Did I not tell you, 'Do not sin against the boy'; and you would not listen? Now comes the <u>reckoning</u> for his blood."" (Gen. 42:42, NAS emphasis added)

The reckoning for his blood in this context does not demand death; reckoning determines what the punishment will be for the blood already shed.

This word 'require' *durash* does not mean to kill or to take a life. This is evident from verse 4 where God instructs Noah that he was permitted to eat any flesh, but the blood shall not be eaten. If 'require' means to kill, why is the animal's blood still 'required' after the beast is already dead? In other words, the animal is already dead when the blood is 'required', so it cannot mean 'to kill'.

The word 'require' here indicates that after death, the blood is 'required', that is, inspected. The blood is required for inspection, reserved for inspection or held for inspection.

PURPOSE FOR INQUISITION

God's Word gives us the reasons why He evaluates the blood of the dead.

BLOOD OF ANIMAL SACRIFICES

This was depicted even in Noah's day with the offering of specified animals, which the Lord called "clean". (8:20) In this context, God had chosen specific kinds of animals that were ceremonially clean, such as oxen, sheep goats and birds. The kind of animal and its health, determined suitability for sacrifice.

BLOOD OF THE RIGHTEOUS AND THE WICKED

In Psalms 9:12 we read that God remembers those who dwell in Zion, when He makes inquisition for blood. (This is the same word used for 'require' in Ge. 9:5) The word for 'remember' means to 'mark out so as to recognize'. The inhabitants of Zion are God's people. (Psa.87; Heb.12:22, 23) Only those who have been marked with the sinless blood of Christ, pass God's inspection.

Respect for Abel's Offering

God had respect for Abel's offering but had no respect for Cain's. Abel offered an animal sacrifice in which blood was shed. Cain offered the fruit of the ground. The word 'respect' means to gaze upon. When God gazed upon Abel's offering, He inspected it, and found it acceptable because of his faith. (Gen.4:2-5; Heb. 11:4)

SUMMARY

God did not command Noah to kill anyone. Neither did God command Noah to inspect blood. God reserves this work for Himself. God looks upon the blood that was shed by the priest. God "requires" blood. God inspects the life represented by shed blood.

5. God's Three Inspections

The teaching of verse five and six is missed if we do not stay with the context of Noah's sacrifice and the actual meaning of the word translated 'require'. God does three examinations. Since the 'shedding of blood' means the loss of life, and the 'life of the flesh is in the blood', God's examinations pertain to the life lived before blood was shed. (Lev. 17:11)

God's allegorical inspection depict His real inspections. (9:5)

- He inspects the lifeblood of your lives. (without 'hand')
- He inspects the lifeblood at or from the hand of every beast **and** from or at the hand of man.
- He inspects the life of man from the hand of every man's brother.

It is significant that the word 'hand' only appears in the second and third inspections. In the second examination, the conjunction 'and' is used to couple 'beast' and 'man'.

The manifestation of death in these sacrifices sets a somber tone for inspection. The blood of animals had been shed. They had died and while the offerings were still smoldering, God gives Noah added insight regarding these three blood examinations.

UNIVERSAL EXAMINATION

The first examination pertained to the life of all mankind.
'And surely the blood of your lives will I inspect...' (9:5a)

THE MEANS OF EXAMINATION

This examination is not merely a ceremony at the blood sacrifice of an animal. Mankind is inducted into this examination by means of death. Those who died in the Flood kept God's appointed time for death, as will everyone after. But that isn't the end. 'It's appointed unto man once to die and after that the judgment.' (Heb.9:27) This inspection pertains to judgment of sin.

THE OBJECT OF EXAMINATION

The object of God's inspection was always the blood of mankind, which represented the life he had lived on earth. God continues to examine the life of man by means of blood. (8:21)

THE REASON FOR THIS EXAMINATION

The reason for man's inspection is his own sin. (Ge. 6:5) Though God promised that He would not curse the earth again with a Flood, mankind's imagination of the heart is still evil from youth. (8:21) Because Noah and his descendants were sinners, God warns him that they were still subject to evaluation.

THE TIME OF THIS EXAMINATION

When the animal was sacrificed, its blood was shed as the visible evidence of death. Like the animals, all mankind would have a postmortem blood inspection.

THE CERTAINTY OF THE EXAMINATION

The writer of Genesis states that this is an absolute certainty. Despite a century of sermons, Noah's message was thought to be a hoax. They thought the Flood and the rain would never happen. As certainly as the lives of Noah's generation were examined, He would most certainly also judge the lifeblood of all mankind after the Flood.

CONSEQUENCE FOR FAILING THE INSPECTION

This was not just about losing one's life. Noah informed his generation of the reason for the coming catastrophe. They would die physically because of its wickedness.

Why bother having this examination if people were already dead? Weren't they already punished? 'And surely the blood of your lives will I inspect', indicates that there is another inspection to come and it would occur after death. Loss of life in the Flood was only a foretaste of God's attitude to sin and what man should expect after death. After death, the sin of mankind is still exposed to a just and holy God, with no power to escape.

The process of dying was the easy part. Enduring the inspection and the consequences after is the dreadful part.

WHAT CAN THE SINNER DO?

God has seen everything. Not only does He see what we do, He reads our minds. (6:5) Immediately after man is done this life on earth, he is subject to an intensely personal examination. Like the antediluvians, succeeding generations will also be held accountable for all the sin God sees in His examination. He misses nothing!

Without exception, God will examine everyone's lifeblood. This is devastating news. Man has no means, no power to shield himself from the piercing rays of God's justice and his wrath against sin. The sinner can do nothing.

Yet, the following examinations enlighten us to how man might escape this examination.

THE ALLEGORICAL EXAMINATION

Most think that the 'good' will out-weigh the bad. This doesn't work, because God can't excuse sin or ignore it, as Adam's generation found out too late.

But again God points the sinner to a means by which he could avert the disastrous consequences of having his 'lifeblood' examined. Depicted by a blood ritual, God teaches the principles of grace.

It's recorded in the middle of the verse where He says,

> 'at the hand of every beast will I inspect it and at the hand of man...' (9:5b)

Noah was the 'man' and the offering was the 'beast'.

TWO 'HANDS'

It is vital to observe the word 'hand' in this verse. Unfortunately, various translations exclude this word.

'Hand' is defined as open hand signifying, power, means or direction. The Interlinear along with the NKJV translates this as 'from the hand'. In this context, 'hands' indicates defensive strength and motion or work to perform a specific task.

In Genesis 9:2, Noah is told that all flesh is delivered into his hand. It is by man's power that they are killed and eaten. (9:3) God tells Cain that that the earth has received his brother's blood from his hand. This implies both power and means. (4:10)

God makes this examination via the 'hand' of every suitable kind of beast and by the 'hand' of man. Since beasts do not have hands, this must be a figurative application. (9:5)[4]

These 'hands' depict the work of divine intervention on man's behalf, by both the priest and the sacrifice. God explains that He would examine the lifeblood of a priest and offering by the power and means of two 'hands'. How could these two 'hands' be the means by which God would be satisfied and expiate sin? Would these two 'hands' have the power to shield sinful man from the wrath of God?

This Hand Has the Power of Intervention

The examination in the first phrase, 'surely the blood of your lives will I inspect', man is left without the power to prevent an inspection and the consequences. He is unprotected.

Because the word 'hand' applies to both the animal sacrificed and the man who sacrificed it, God intended to teach the worshipper that this power to deflect the wrath of God against sin must reside in both the priest and the sacrifice. They must both be 'clean'. The work of the hand of both priest and sacrifice are essential elements of the priesthood.

REASON FOR ANOTHER INSPECTION

If the first inspection were not a reality, there would be no reason to portray this second examination to reveal the third. The first reason for this inspection was to portray how man's sin had left him exposed to God's justice. The second reason is to depict God's remedy by the death of an innocent animal.

The 'hand' of beast and the 'hand' of man illustrate that the application of blood is work. God gave specific instructions for the preparation of the priestly ministry. They were to bathe before and wear garments that minimized sweat. (Lev. 16:4,24; Ezek.44:18)

---

[4] The NAS and ESV do not have the word 'hand'. For correct translation see KJV, NKJV and YLT along with an Interlinear Hebrew.

Only the work of a Priest who was perfect in every way would be acceptable before a Holy God. (Lk. 22:44)

THE MEANING OF 'EVERY'

'Every' means 'whole, every, any or all'. Obviously, God is not demanding that Noah eat every single moving thing. (9:3) He simply granted man permission to kill and eat **any** living thing.

'Every Beast' But Not 'Every Man' (9:5b)

Still in the context of the sacrifice, "every beast" signifies God's inspection of **any** appropriate "clean" beast used in sacrifice. It could not be just any animal. Noah could select any or every beast designated suitable for sacrifice, that is, 'clean'. (8:20; 9:5) Scripture specifies goats, sheep and cattle among others suitable for sacrifice.

But this does not say "every man". There is only one kind of 'man' to make the sacrifice: a human being. This would not be an angel or any other kind of being. A man was required to sacrifice the animal.

For millennia God would symbolically examine the shed blood of every sacrificed 'beast' and the lifeblood of the priest. There was to be an organic holy harmony in the work of priest and sacrifice.

MEANS OF INSPECTION

Noah knew that Cain's offering was rejected. He knew that God accepted Abel's sacrifice. He knew that only by the shedding of innocent blood could fellowship with God be restored. The means of deliverance from the wrath of God was by means of death, a substitutionary death depicted by a suitable animal, sacrificed by a suitable man.

The blood of both the sacrifice and the priest were symbolically inspected according to God's requirements. Both of them represented the work of God.

PLACE OF INSPECTION

The examination of the blood of both offering and priest is at the altar. An efficacious remedy is pictured as a meeting of both priest and sacrifice in the presence of God at the altar.

RITUAL IS REPEATED

There was still a problem. Though God had instituted the sacerdotal system, this repeatable ritual could only illustrate the necessity for man's deliverance from inevitable failure to meet God's righteous standards. If these ceremonies had been effective, they would not need to be repeated.

Yet, this ritual continued to serve as a temporary symbolic lens through which God would view His final examination. Somehow both the 'hand' of beast and 'hand' of man must be united to protect man from the wrath of God in that first inspection. This means of examination ceremonially illustrated the power of a righteous blood sacrifice shed by a perfect man as eternal protection and ultimate deliverance from the wrath of God.

But Noah knew from Gen. 3:15 that a repeatable ritual was not what God had promised in his Covenant.

ONE FINAL EXAMINATION

We come now to the third examination, 'from the hand of every man's brother will I examine the life of man.' (9:5c)

In this inspection there is no beast. Every man's life will still be examined. This inspection will occur from the hand of every man's brother. With the word 'brother', God is referring to one person. He does **not** say every man's 'brothers.'

GOD INSPECTS EVERY MAN'S BROTHER

With the animal sacrifices, God taught us that we need both a priest and a sacrifice to deal with our sins. But in this third examination only the hand of every man's brother is referenced. God will also inspect the life of man from the 'hand of every man's brother', one man. Who is he?

WHO IS EVERY MAN'S BROTHER?

Scripture specifically informs us who every man's brother is.

The Meaning Of 'Brother'

The word 'brother' in this passage denotes relationship. However, 'brother' does not necessarily refer to an immediate relative. The

Hebrew word includes the idea of affinity or resemblance. Had it been written that the blood of a **certain** man's brother was to be inspected, we would understand from the context that they were immediate relatives. However, it is written that from the hand of **every** man's brother, I will inspect the life of man. We are informed here that every man has a brother. Unlike sacrificed animals this man is our brother in the flesh.

Christ Is Identified As 'Brother' According To The Flesh.

James is identified as the Lord's brother in the flesh. (Gal.1:19; 1 Cor. 9:5)

Christ Is Identified As The Believers' Brother

Jesus said that those who do the will of God are His brothers. (Mk. 3:35) After His resurrection Jesus calls His disciples 'brothers'. (Jn. 20:17) 'Every man's brother' is a prophetic reference to our Lord, who would reveal Himself in flesh and become our Substitute for sin. The author of Hebrews speaks of Christ declaring His name to his brothers and that He is not ashamed to call us brothers!! (Heb. 2:11,12) So, it was necessary that there would be One who could be 'every man's brother'.

Every Man's Brother

Who is every man's brother in Genesis? In the previous examination, a living priest offered the blood of a dead animal. Now in this third inspection, there is certainly no blood of any dead animal. There is only one man, a living man and brother.

SUMMARY

Again, God's examinations are three-fold. God will make personal inspection of everyone's life, represented in this narrative by blood. God would examine the blood of the 'hand' of the priest and the blood of the 'hand' of the animal as a ceremonial depiction of the means necessary to justly satisfy God's wrath against us. In this third examination God would inspect the blood of man by means (hand) of every man's Brother. (Gen. 9:4,5)

The next verse explains why Christ could be our Substitute.

6. THE SACRIFICE AND PRIEST

The ceremonial shedding of animal blood became a regular expected practice in the worship of God. Yet, the sacrifice of an innocent animal for man's sin was only a portrayal of the huge cost God would have to pay for the salvation of His people.

God explained to Noah what He did with the sacrifices and what he expected from them. He was informed that the means by which God determined to examine man's lifeblood is by priest and sacrifice. Lastly, God apprised Noah that He would examine the blood of every man's brother. This meant that a man's innocent blood would have to be shed. (9:5)

THE SACRIFICE

Noah now knows that a man will have to die as a sacrifice. In the context of Priest and sacrifice, he would wonder who would shed this man's blood. God tells him.

> "Whoever sheds man's blood, by man his blood shall be shed; for in the image of God made He man." (Gen.9:6 NKJV)

God says plainly that man's blood shall be shed by man!

THE SHEDDING OF BLOOD

The Hebrew word used in 9:6 for 'shed' means to spill, to expend life, gush or pour out, or libation. Though the word 'shed' also applies to the act of murder elsewhere in Scripture, this context precludes that meaning.[5] God spoke this to Noah in a worship service.

The 'shedding of blood' can only refer to that which is sacrificed. The same word 'shed' is also translated as 'poured'. (De. 12:27) This

---

[5] The word for 'shed' in Hebrew has different meanings depending on context. See *Shedding Blood* in Notes

is the pouring out of life's blood in libation because of a divine obligation.

Man's Blood

The 'blood' of verse 6 cannot be separated from the last phrase of the previous verse, 'I will inspect the life of man'. Again, before the inspection takes place a death must occur.

The Source of Blood

The source of the blood is the 'life of man', not an animal. (Heb. 9:12)

Why Man's Blood

'Every man' applies to everyone who had lived and everyone who would yet live. According to the flesh, this Man is a brother to all, therefore making His sacrifice applicable to humanity.

The Blood Must Atone

The shedding of blood of the sacrifice signified death, physical death. The writer of Hebrews informs us with OT symbolism, that without the shedding of blood there is no remission of sins. (Heb. 9:22) But it is not only the act of sacrifice that is important here; it is what the blood itself represents.

> "For the life of the flesh is in the blood, and I have given
> it to you upon the altar to make atonement for your souls;
> for it is the blood that makes atonement for the soul."
> (Lev.17:11, NKJV)

The shedding of blood represents the death necessary for man's atonement; the blood represents the life of the one who died. To permanently propitiate for man's sins a man's blood sacrifice was needed.

The Blood Must Nourish

Blood was shed in order that His children could be sustained with the spiritual nourishment needed to live with Him forever. (Jn. 6:53) Having been lethally poisoned by the fruit of the tree of knowledge of good and evil, we have been barred from life. The only antidote for that poison is the blood of Christ. We now consume fruit from another tree, the cross upon which Christ had offered His body and shed His blood, which came from a perfect life. We remember this fact every time we partake at the Lord's Table and drink of the fruit of the vine. There is only one life, one blood from which we spiritually partake and that is the blood of Christ.

SUMMARY

Though there are several ways that 'shed' is used, this context only allows one meaning. Since the explicit statements in this passage do not even imply that a murder occurred, 'shed' here could only mean blood that had been poured out in sacrifice. The shedding of blood in Genesis 9:6 indicates that a human sacrifice was essential for the salvation of His people.

But that wasn't all.

THE PRIEST

Who is to shed man's blood? '**By man must his blood be shed**' Again, as we keep the context in mind, we see Noah stand before the altar and make a blood sacrifice. He is the priest but not a sacrifice. (9:6)

Noah knew that God performed the first sacrifices when animal skins were provided for Adam and Eve. Likely performed by the pre-incarnate Christ, the death of the Lamb of God to come must be performed by Man. He must be Adam-like. He must be a man.

The one to shed the blood of the Man could not be an angel because angels are not created in the image of God.

God had indicated to Satan that He would bruise the heel of the Seed but Satan also could not shed this Man's blood.

'By man must his blood be shed' indicates that a man must serve as this priest. Since animal sacrifice was not sufficient, it was necessary that a man's blood be shed. God made it clear that man's blood was required, but who would shed that man's blood? The answer is clear. Adam (man) would be shedding the blood of Adam. (Gen. 9:6) The first Adam had died a sinner. Obviously, it was impossible that he be that man.

'Whoever' is a Man

The one who sheds man's blood must be a man! (Ge. 9:6)

'Whoever" is Every Man's Brother

He is every man's Brother. (v. 5) He is related to mankind in the flesh.

'Whoever' is a Priest

Whoever sheds man's blood in this setting is a Priest. God is referencing another priesthood, which did not pertain to the sacrifice of animals and most certainly not murder. (Heb. 4:14-16)

He must have an everlasting priesthood. (Heb. 3:20)

He must finish his work with one sacrifice.

> "But this Man, after He had offered one sacrifice for sins forever, sat down at the right hand of God ..." (Heb. 10:12)

Jesus was this Man, the Priest, who offered a Man for the sins of mankind. He was not a victim!

> Therefore My Father loves Me, because I lay down my life that I may take it again. No one takes it from Me, but I lay it down of Myself. I have power to lay it down and I have power to take it again." (Jn.10:17,18a; NKJ)

The blood shed by this priest is shed for others.

> This cup is the new testament in my blood, which is shed for you." (Lk. 22:20)

Both the Priest and the Sacrifice purge sins.

> "How much more shall the blood of Christ, who through the eternal Spirit, offered Himself without spot to God, purge your conscience from dead works to serve the living God?" (Heb. 9:14)

This Priest shed this Man's blood by laying down His own life.

The Promise

Again, 'Whoever sheds man's blood, by man shall his blood be shed; for in the image of God made he man.' Moses informs us of how the promise would be fulfilled and the reason it was possible.

It was a twofold fulfillment. Man's blood would need to be poured out, and Man would shed that blood.

This "Man" must be our High Priest to offer Himself as that one necessary Sacrifice sufficient to save His people. (Heb.7:26,27)

This Man has no beast to offer because He was both the Priest and the Sacrifice! Genesis 9:5,6 point ahead to the glorious fact that another Adam would come to shed His precious blood and thus be the means by which He could be our Substitute. As both the Priest and the Sacrifice, He had the power to satisfy God's inspection on our behalf. To escape the first inspection, man must be covered with His blood.

THIS IS THE PROMISED COVENANT

To atone for the sins of man, it was necessary to shed man's blood, not animal. Secondly, this man's blood would need to be shed by man. God promised Noah that the ultimate sacrifice requires the shedding of the blood of one Man's blood by Man. This is exactly what happened.

This Man could not be prevented by death to be our everlasting Priest. (Heb. 7:23) Jesus tells us that His blood is shed for us. He is the one who has the power to lay down his life and to take it up again. As our High Priest, He lays down his life to shed His own blood. Unlike the animal sacrifices, this sacrifice was offered by Man only once and without 'spot' or 'deformity'.

The Man's blood that was shed for us is Jesus Christ. The Man who offered this Sacrifice is Jesus Christ. The One who shed this Man's blood is the same Person: He is Jesus Christ our Great High Priest! Therefore, 'Whoever sheds Christ's blood, by Christ will His blood be shed.'

This is God's Covenant He made for Adam and Eve and confirmed to Noah.

The Sacrifice and the Priest are the same Man. He is every man's Brother.

7. THE IMAGE OF GOD

Sacrifice on behalf of mankind is linked to one vital fact - that man was made in the image of God. Both Priest and Sacrifice were the same person and identified as Man, as Genesis 9:6 points out.

But there is another important factor essential to ministry of our High Priest. Had man not been made in the image of God, saving him from sin would be impossible. "For in the image of God made he man".

Christ is the 'express image' of His Person thus able to purge man's sins. (Heb. 1:3) There is only one original image. Man was **not** created as another image of God; man was created in that image. We might say that He is the mold of which there is only one. Mankind was cast from that single mold.

It should be noted that angels also have intellect, emotions and a will. After all, it was Lucifer who by his own 'free will' rebelled against God. To assert free will as a feature of the image of God is serious error. Even God does not have a free will! Our High Priest did not have a free will! It is impossible for God to decide to sin! On the other hand, man, who is born in sin, is only capable of deciding according to his nature. Being sinful, man's 'freewill' precludes any righteous choices. Though man was created sinless, he was not created righteous. The righteousness of God is everlasting. (Psa.119:137,142) Indeed, man was created with the potential for righteousness, but that was not the image in which he was created.

However there is one aspect of His image essential for the work of the Priest and the Sacrifice.

THE IMAGE OF SURVIVAL

No doubt, Noah thought of the animal sacrifices God made for Adam and Eve, but even these divine sacrifices were insufficient. Animals were not made in the image of God, therefore could only portray a substitutionary sacrifice for sin. There was nothing about them that would live after death.

Similarly, angels were also not created in the image of God because they had no life to give. Nothing about them could die and live again, so they would also be disqualified as a sacrifice.

Having this created nature to die and survive, man has the potential of redemption, if a suitable substitute could be found. Man needed the sacrifice by the Man and of the Man in whose image he had been created. He can be rescued by the One in whose image he had been created. Had man not been able to survive death, substitutionary atonement would not have been possible. He would then have been in the same predicament as fallen angels – unredeemable! To be created in the image of God means that man must be able to survive death.

The survival rate of the human race is 100%! For man then, the issue of his survival is how he will fare in God's blood examinations.

OUR SUBSTITUTE MUST BE A MAN

Since man has been created in His image, God tells Noah that a Man must sacrifice this Man. (9:6) So, His image was revealed to us through Christ in the 'fullness of time' with a prepared body. (Gal. 4:4, Heb. 10:5)

He Must Be Able To Survive Death

This man would be the one in whose image we have been created. He would be able to survive death. (Jn. 10:17, 18) 'The one who sheds man's blood, must be shed by man for in the image of God made he man,' is a promise that one day a Priest would come who could offer one last Sacrifice – Himself. Christ as our Sacrifice experienced physical death, but Christ, the Priest did not die. He did not cease to exist!

His Blood Must Be Able To Restore Fellowship

Alienated from God, man had no means of restoring fellowship. Divine examination of man's blood would not miss the slightest contamination. Little sins or big sins, man is naturally an enemy of God. Only by means of pure and undefiled blood, could reconciliation with God be restored. Indeed, by making His peace available for man through the blood of the cross, He accomplished exactly that. (Col. 1:20-22)

Man Needed a Mediator

Jesus was the Mediator of this New Covenant. (Heb. 8:6; 9:15) The writer of Hebrews refers to the necessity of a spiritual sprinkling of the conscience from dead works to serve the living God. (Heb. 9:14) Jesus sprinkled us with His cleansing blood as typified by Moses, when he sprinkled blood on the people. (Heb.9:19,20; 1 Pe. 1:2)

It was shed for the remission of sins. (Matt. 26:28) His blood purges the conscience. (Heb. 9:14) His blood redeems us. (1 Pet. 1:18,19) His blood washes us from our sins. (1 Jn. 1:7; Rev. 1:5; 7:14) It justifies us and atones for our sin. (Rom. 5:9)

SUMMARY

The substitutionary death of Christ would be impossible if we had not been created in the image of God. This Man's blood was shed by Man for mankind. The ultimate Sacrifice had to be made by someone who could be our Substitute, who was both sinless and righteous! We exult in the fact that the blood of every man's Brother has been examined and found to be without blemish! Our Righteous Priest offered one Righteous Sacrifice!

Because God has created man in His image, it was possible for Him to provide Man as a Substitute who would not only die but also survive it. Every person, whether a believer or not, carries this image of God. A few will survive death with Christ while the vast majority will survive death without Him. (Jn. 5:29; 1 Cor.15:35, 36, 51)

When God 'smelled a soothing aroma', He was thinking about every man's Brother who would come as both the Priest and Sacrifice to permanently atone for the sins of His people by dying and rising from the dead. Only by one pure and holy Sacrifice could God permanently expiate the obnoxious stench of sin and smell a soothing aroma instead.

8. The Two Covenants

God had told Noah before and after the Deluge that He would confirm "My Covenant" with him.

There are two covenants. Adam and Eve were enlisted in the first Covenant before they had sinned. When they disobeyed God, they broke the bilateral Covenant God had made with them. Thankfully, God had also instituted a unilateral Covenant on man's behalf.

COVENANT OF WORKS

When instructed not to eat the fruit from the tree of the knowledge of good and evil, it appears that Adam and Eve had every intention of complying with God's request. They did not make plans to disobey God. The contract was simple: don't eat the forbidden fruit and you will not die; eat the forbidden fruit and you will die. Imminent death was the incentive to defer to other fruit. If man complied, God would continue to honor the terms of the covenant he made with man - man would not die. Adam and Eve had to work to keep their part of the Covenant. (Ge. 2:17; 6:7-13) This was a Covenant of Works.

TEMPTED WITH A 'BETTER' OPTION

However, Satan deceived Adam and Eve by telling them that they would know good and evil if they ate of the forbidden fruit. (6:18) At the point they believed Satan and desired the fruit, they had to eat the fruit. Life had been great in Eden, but in that split second everything changed.

They would be as gods! 'How much better it would be if we could know for ourselves what good and evil is', so they thought. They disobeyed God by following the advice of His enemy. Now, man had indeed made themselves gods, doing whatever he thought was right in his own eyes. (Ge. 3:22; 8:21; Judges 21:25) Satan had introduced Adam and Eve to the doctrine of 'self-esteem'.

Locked into God's Covenant of righteous Laws that cannot be kept or abrogated, man would have no means of avoiding the dire consequences, without divine intervention.

THE COVENANT VIA MT. SINAI

God had brought the children of Israel out of the land of bondage. At Mt. Sinai, God tells Moses to ask Israel if they were interested in a covenant, 'My Covenant'. If Israel could fulfill the obligations of this contract, they would be a peculiar people. (Ex. 19:5, 6) Moses presented God's contract offer to the elders of the people. All the people were of one voice, saying, 'All that the Lord commands us we will do.' Who wouldn't want to be special among all people? (Ex. 30:6-8)

The Covenant was "made" with Israel in Horeb. (De. 5:2) 'Made' denotes a formal induction into a covenant by passing between halved animal carcasses. This Covenant was to be kept. (Ex. 19:5; De. 5:1)

Well, the day came when they would hear the voice of the Lord. But as they heard God speak, with all the audio visuals of smoke, thunder and lightening, the noise of the trumpet, they backed away from the mountain, way back! They pleaded with Moses that he speak God's words to them instead, and they would hear. (Ex. 20:1,18, 19; De. 5:22) They formally entered into a covenant of works with God.

But, while Moses was up on the Mount getting the Commandments inscribed in stone, God told him to get back down to the people where they were dancing around a golden calf that Aaron had helped them build. It didn't take them long to exhibit their utter inability to keep His Covenant. (Ex. 32)

Man's first parents enrolled their descendants in a works contract with God. Born sinners, man will inevitably fail. No amount of good intentions and self-effort will succeed in honoring this first Covenant. If man doesn't get into the other Covenant, he is doomed.

COVENANT OF PROMISE

Like the Covenant at Mt. Sinai, the Covenant given to Noah is also called, "My Covenant". God initiated both of them; both of them required God's righteousness. Unable to keep his first Covenant with God, man needed another Covenant.

WHERE WAS THIS COVENANT MADE?

God was establishing or confirming a covenant to Noah that had already been made. This covenant corresponds to the one given in the Garden of Eden after Adam and Eve sinned. (Gen.3:15) This was God's solution to the failure of Adam and Eve to abide by the terms of the first Covenant. Different than the first Covenant, God not only initiated it, He alone expedited it.

THE GOSPEL COVENANT OF PROMISE WAS PLANNED

With God, the redemption of a fallen race was not an after-thought, thinking 'Oh my, Adam has sinned we need to do something.' Intentionally created in His image, God had made it possible to make Himself a Substitute for man. It was all planned from before the world began. The Lamb of God was slain from the foundation of the world. (Rev.13:8) Our great salvation was not 'plan B'. (Ac.2:23,24)

God initiated two Covenants. But one was the reason for the other. Which Covenant was God establishing with Noah?

SUMMARY

Paul speaks of two covenants. One pertains to the works of the Law and the other pertains to the hearing of faith. (Ga. 2:16; 3:2) He likens the Covenants to two sons, two women and two cities. (Ga. 4:21-31) Ishmael, born of Hagar the bondwoman, represented a covenant of the works of the flesh. Isaac, born of Sarah, represented a covenant of promise, which Paul refers to as the Seed. (Ga. 3:16) The Covenant pertaining to Sarah could be none other than the Seed of Gen. 3:15. One Covenant pertains to an earthly Jerusalem; the other Covenant pertains to heavenly Jerusalem.

God's holiness does not permit Him to cancel His Covenant of Works containing His righteous laws. It has not been revised neither can it be abrogated.

The only means by which God can liberate us from the demands of the first contract is by death. Paul compares this to God's law of marriage that cannot be abrogated. By Law the only way a woman is free to remarry is if her husband dies. (Rom 7:1-6) Likewise, if man could die and be made a new creature in Christ, he would no longer be under its penalty. (2 Cor.5:17)

Indeed, the one who has been relieved of his obligation under the Covenant of Works has died! Only by being crucified with Christ can man be released from the obligations of the Covenant of Works for salvation. (Ga.2:20) The man or woman of faith sees Jesus to be his or her one and only perfect Sacrifice for sin.

Noah shed the blood of an innocent animal as an act of faith that he needed a substitutionary sacrifice. Noah had found grace in the eyes of the Lord with the same Covenant of Grace Paul explained in the New Testament.

Paul identified the Seed promised to Adam and Eve as a Covenant. Having gleaned his insight by the Holy Spirit from the OT, the Apostle would have understood the meaning of 'established' and 'establishing' 'The Covenant', or 'My Covenant' as discussed in the following chapter.

9. The Gospel Covenant

Believing God's warning of an impending Deluge, Noah built the ark, as he was instructed. (Heb.11:7) Not only did God warn Noah of His plan, He explained that He was confirming 'My Covenant'. (6:18)

THE SOOTHING AROMA

Now, over a century after he started building the ark, it came to rest on Mt Ararat. What would be the first thing Noah and his family did after they disembarked?

NOAH'S WORSHIP

Noah knew that God was offended by the pervasive wicked thoughts and deeds of His creation, and for that reason He fulfilled His justified judgment of mankind. (6:1-7) This had been a generation of self-worshippers.

Noah knew that he was a sinner like all those who perished in the Flood. He also knew he could not satisfy God's anger against his own sin, unless innocent blood was shed on his behalf. He therefore built an altar and sacrificed specific animals he knew would be acceptable to God. By this he personally demonstrated that his dependence for salvation from the wrath of God, could not rest upon his works. He worshipped God by his faith in God.

It was on this occasion that God makes an astonishing statement. With the death of all mankind and animals on earth still fresh in the minds of Noah and his family, God smelled a soothing aroma! How could that be? What was that aroma about?

APPEASING GOD'S ANGER

Was God's anger now appeased because He had eliminated the source of His grief? Was the burning of the sacrifices soothing to God because He had just destroyed mankind with the exception of Noah and his family? But the destruction of humanity certainly couldn't have been the reason for the 'fragrant aroma', because God knew that man, still being naturally evil, would continue to produce a progeny of sinners, the same as before. A character reformation was out of the question. (8:21) Man's dogged lust for sin would continue to expose him to God's wrath. Though God would still use famine, pestilence and even wars to mitigate persistent evil in the world, never would He flood the earth again. (Ezek. 14:12-21) (8:22)

Knowing that man's wickedness would be replicated, the Deluge could not have been reason for the 'soothing aroma'. God does not take pleasure in the death of the wicked. (Ez.18:32; 33:11)

COMMANDED TO MULTIPLY

Despite His knowledge that wickedness would proliferate again, God still blessed Noah and his sons by telling them to multiply, as He had Adam and Eve. (1:28; 9:1) How could God refrain from exacting justice upon the next generation, which would be no better than Adam's?

SUMMARY

The answer is the 'fragrant aroma'.

Amazingly, it was during Noah's offering that God smelled a soothing aroma. (8:21) God had blessed Noah and his sons with a command to be fruitful and multiply **after** He had 'smelled a soothing aroma'. While Noah smelled burning flesh from the offering, God smelled the fragrance of the offering of every man's Brother by a perfect Priest. (Heb. 10:6) He would be satisfied in the death of this one Righteous Man, never the death of the wicked.

'MY COVENANT'

The common interpretation of the rainbow 'covenant' is that God simply promised never to cause another Deluge. But of what value is such a 'covenant'? While Noah is making the sacrifice, God tells Noah that though the heart of man is evil from his youth, He would not destroy the earth with a flood again. (8:21) That's good! But, despite this great Flood, nothing has changed in the heart of man! His nature is the same as before. What consolation is it to know that mankind will not be inundated with water again, if judgment is coming after death anyway? Unless the heart of man could be dealt with there is no solace in this news. This promise is good only for as long as the earth remains, till God destroyed the earth by some other means. (8:22) Is that really all there is to the Covenant God established with Noah?

Only One Covenant

The term 'covenant' occurs eight times pertaining to the Flood. (Ge. 6:18; 9:9, 11, 12, 13, 15, 16, 17) Whether they are termed "My" or "the", they are singular, indicating they refer to the same covenant. However, on different occasions 'My Covenant' is established.

'MY COVENANT' IS CONFIRMED

The word translated 'establish' means to confirm, 'make clearer' or continue something that already existed, in this case 'My Covenant'. It does not mean that God would craft another brand-new covenant. But their contexts indicate ways in which God establishes the Covenant He had already unilaterally made to Adam and Eve after they sinned. (Gen. 3:15) He continued to clarify it or establish it with supplementary events and promises.

'I Will Establish My Covenant' (6:18)

When Noah received instructions for the Ark, God said that He will confirm "My Covenant" with or 'near' or alongside Noah and his family. (Gen. 6:18) The word 'with', in this context, cannot mean that God entered into a bilateral agreement with Noah.

Grieved with man's sinful condition, God in His holiness sighed deeply (repented) about having created man on the earth. (6:6) Had man been able to restrain his wickedness there would have been no need for God to 'establish' His Covenant to Adam and Eve by preserving Noah, his family and a pair of each kind of animal, while destroying all the rest of man and animals on earth. (6:5-7) By preserving Noah and his family, God demonstrated how important it was to confirm that a preexisting Covenant, made to Adam and Eve, must still be ratified. (Gen. 3:15)

'I Am Establishing My Covenant' (9:9)

After the Flood God says, 'I am confirming My Covenant.' Literally, 'I confirm My Covenant near you and near your descendants after you.' (9:9, 10)

> "And lo, I am establishing My Covenant with you, and with your seed after you," (Gen. 9:9, Young's Literal Translation.)

This implies that God's continuing action was needed not to eradicate everyone with a deluge again, though they deserved it.

I Will Establish (9:11)

By this confirmation of 'My Covenant', God assured mankind that it would be fulfilled. (Gen.3:15) Furthermore, God also assured mankind that He would not flood the earth again.

Another 'Establish' Example

God also promised Abraham that He would 'establish' "My Covenant" with his wife Sarah's son, not Hagar's son, thus providing another indicator in this Covenant's progress to its consummation in Christ's Priesthood. (Gen. 17:19, 21)

SUMMARY

The Flood, the preservation of Noah's family, His promise not to flood the earth again, and the sign of the rainbow were the first confirmations of His Covenant. These were new confirmations of 'My Covenant', not new covenants.

Covenant Confirmed For People And Animals

God confirmed 'My Covenant' for you and for Noah's descendants. As descendants of Noah, this includes us today. The Covenant is for sinners and is confirmed for sinners. (9:9)

God also confirms His Covenant 'near' or alongside the animals for man's sake. The animals that died in the Flood, of course, were unable to process reasons for their calamity. Innocent animals suffered in death because of man's sin. Another confirmation of

'My Covenant' included a promise that God would never again cause a Deluge to decimate animals because of man's guilt. (9:10)

'My Covenant' Propitiated For Mankind

Man's belligerent inability to satisfy God's holy standard left him in a dreadful state. Yet God graciously confirmed 'My Covenant' by promising not to destroy the world again because of His mercy, not because the world deserved another chance. All mankind, those who worshipped God, and those who didn't, would benefit from the confirmation of His Covenant.

For indeed, 'He is the propitiation for our sins and not for our sins only but for the sins of the whole world.' (1 Jn.2:2) The world at large would be shielded from God's anger temporarily, for His saints, it was permanent. The primary purpose for God's mercy to the whole world was to glorify Himself by having an elect people with whom He would no longer be angry. (Isa. 54:9)

THE SIGN OF THE GOSPEL COVENANT

God told Noah that He would confirm the Covenant by 'appointing' a bow between heaven and earth, which would be seen in the cloud. Certainly this would mitigate apprehensions in the rainstorms that would follow. But it was much more than that.

THE BOW SIGN

God had confirmed 'My Covenant' to preserve Noah and was confirming His Covenant with a promise not to flood the earth again. (9:8-11) Then God would confirm 'My Covenant' with the sign of the rainbow. The rainbow is the sign of 'My Covenant'. (9:12-17) The sign of the rainbow confirms 'My Covenant' with His promise not to flood the earth again.

The Hebrew word usually translated 'rainbow' should be 'bow'. A bow was used for hunting and war. (Gen. 27:3; 48:22)

The Rainbow Sign is 'Between'

Neither the word 'with' or 'between' state or imply a bilateral agreement between God and man. The rainbow was appointed to be a sign between God and man, throughout his generations. (9:12)

God is above, and man is on earth below. 'Between' denotes a spatial perspective. The rainbow is between heaven where God is and earth, where man is.[6] (9:13)

The Covenant Is 'Between'.

Just as the rainbow is between heaven and earth, so also is 'My Covenant'. 'Remember' means to mark or to recognize.[7] When God sees the rain-bow, He recognizes that His only reason for not flooding the world again is 'My Covenant'. The rain-bow is the "sign of the covenant" between heaven and earth, between God and man. (9:12, 13) It was and is this Covenant that shielded and is shielding the world from God's wrath.

When God sees the rainbow, He remembers the reason why He is not flooding the earth again – 'My Covenant'.

THE GOSPEL COVENANT

His promise not to flood the earth was a new confirmation of 'My Covenant'. (9:11) God remembers 'My Covenant' as the reason why He would not be flooding the earth again. (8:21; 9:6, 15) This rainbow sign was new, the promise not to flood the earth was new, but the Covenant could not have been 'established', if it had not already existed. 'My Covenant' was not new.

THE 'AROMA' WAS NOT A SIGN

The context of 'My Covenant' is that God smelled a soothing aroma. Immediately after the Lord smelled a sweet aroma at Noah's sacrifice He promised not to destroy man again as He had in the Flood. This fragrant aroma is a symbolic description of how God would expedite His Covenant, thus making it possible for Him to withhold his righteous anger and not curse the earth again for man's

---

[6] Examples of Spatial References: Melchizedek and Abram affirmed God as the possessor of heaven and earth. (Ge.14:19,22) The Lord rained brimstone on Sodom from heaven. (19:24) God spoke through an angel from heaven. (21:17) God spoke to Abram out of heaven. (22:11, 15) He is the God of heaven and earth. (24:3)

[7] 'Remember' is an anthropomorphism. Of course, God cannot forget. But it does imply that man forgets the meaning of the rainbow sign.

sake. (8:21) The rainbow sign of 'My Covenant' points to the aromatic satisfactory Sacrifice of every man's Brother.

THE RAINBOW SIGN

Everyone before Christ could know that the rainbow sign confirmed the Covenant that every man's Brother would come to shed His own blood; everyone after Christ could know that the rainbow sign confirmed the fulfillment of that same Covenant at the cross of Christ.

The rainbow is a sign from God that judgment is coming. Unless man agrees with God's list of sins in the Bible, repents from them and turns by faith to Christ, he will be subject to God's personal examination of his 'lifeblood'.

The rainbow sign reminds believers that they have escaped the just punishment for sin by the sacrifice of Christ who is every man's Brother, that no work they had done commended them to God. Having repented of their sin, they have escaped God's Blood Examination Day at the Great White Throne judgment, when God opens each man's memoir for inspection. (Rev. 20:11, 12)

God would inspect the blood of every man's Brother, a Man to come who must be both the Priest and the Sacrifice. (9:5,6) Every man's Brother is none other than God the Son, who became our High Priest to offer Himself as the Sacrifice. Only Christ's sacrifice could be that 'soothing aroma' that God smelled at Noah's sacrifice, that John the Baptist proclaimed as the Lamb of God who takes away the sin of the world. (Matt. 3:17; Jn. 1:29; 2 Pe.1:17) Christ himself was the High Priest who laid His own life down for us upon the altar of the cross. It is this Man who made His own shed blood available to God for examination in place of ours.

Then the rainbow was a sign of the Covenant that had not yet been ratified at the Cross; today it is a sign that the Covenant has been ratified at the Cross. Before and after Christ, the message is the same: God sees the rainbow and remembers 'My Covenant', the soothing aroma, which was the reason why He promised not to curse the earth again. (8:21, 22)

The rainbow is a sign of 'My Covenant'. God had made a Covenant to provide a perfect Priest and a perfect Sacrifice to shed His own blood for our sin! This Gospel of the rainbow sign is the same gospel that the prophets and the apostles preached.

Had there been no soothing aroma, there would be no Covenant of grace through Jesus Christ and no rainbow sign.

The rainbow sign points mankind to God's Covenant promise that 'He who sheds Man's blood, by Man shall His blood be shed.' Or, 'He who sheds Christ's blood, by Christ shall His blood be shed.' This is the gospel of the rainbow sign.

10. Notes

SHEDDING BLOOD

The word shed has different applications, depending on context. 'Shed' means to 'pour' or to 'pour out'.

Shedding Blood Pertains To Murder.

The word used for kill in the Decalogue has to do with murder. However the Hebrew word for "shed" is also used to describe murder. "For their feet run to evil and make haste to shed blood." (Prov. 1:16) Reuben makes a plea for his brothers not to "shed" blood but rather cast Joseph into the pit. (Gen. 37:22) The description of shedding blood given in Psa. 106:35-38 pertains to murder. The Canaanites shed the innocent blood of their sons and daughters by sacrificing them to demons. (Psa. 106:37,38)

Shedding Of Blood Pertains To Manslaughter

Cities of refuge were provided for those who accidentally killed another person. To shed the blood of one who did not intend to kill another was to shed innocent blood. (De.19:10)

God informs David that he can't build the Temple because he has shed much blood. (1 Chr. 22:8; 28:3) Intentional killing in war was not deemed to be murder. This would compare to killing in self-defense.

Shedding Blood Pertains To A Sacrificial Offering

The shedding of blood also is a description of animal sacrifices in the OT. The Levitical priests are given instructions to 'shed' or 'pour' the blood of the animal beside the bottom of the altar. (Ex. 29:12; Lev. 4:7, 18: 4:25, 30, 34) Genesis 9:6 could also be translated, 'Whoever pours man's blood, by man shall his blood be poured'.

To order more copies of this book, find books by other
Canadian authors, or make inquiries about publishing
your own book, contact PageMaster at:

PageMaster Publication Services Inc.
11340-120 Street, Edmonton, AB T5G 0W5
books@pagemaster.ca
780-425-9303

catalogue and e-commerce store
PageMasterPublishing.ca/Shop

ABOUT THE AUTHOR

Raised by Christian parents in conservative churches, Bible teaching has greatly benefited Howard Boldt from childhood. Since Bible College, he served in church administration, music, and teaching Sunday and mid-week Bible classes. With his growing interest in the Scriptures, Howard became particularly concerned about the negative impact doctrinal errors were having upon Christians. From teaching to essays to books, he has attempted to articulate biblical reasoning for his views. Happily married to his wife of 51 years, he has also experienced the joys of family life. He lives in Alberta, Canada.

www.ingramcontent.com/pod-product-compliance
Lightning Source LLC
Chambersburg PA
CBHW071736020426
42331CB00008B/2058